Color Your World Pretty

Meditational Coloring Book Vol(1)

ILLUSTRATIONS BY:

DLDaniels

 www.trafford.com

North America & international
toll-free: 1 888 232 4444 (USA & Canada)
fax: 812 355 4082

Dedication:

I like the dedicate this book to my Beautiful grandmother, who is now
With our heavenly father on the other side of the pearlie-gate, my mother
And sister, brothers and the rest of my family. May God bless us all. Thank you!

15

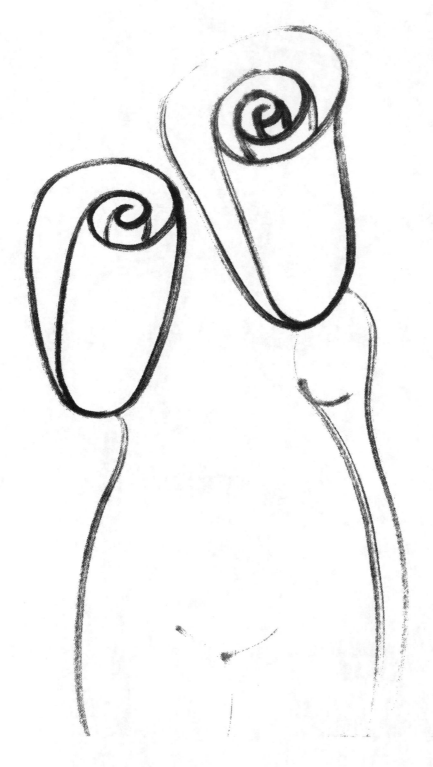

18

20

34

38

49

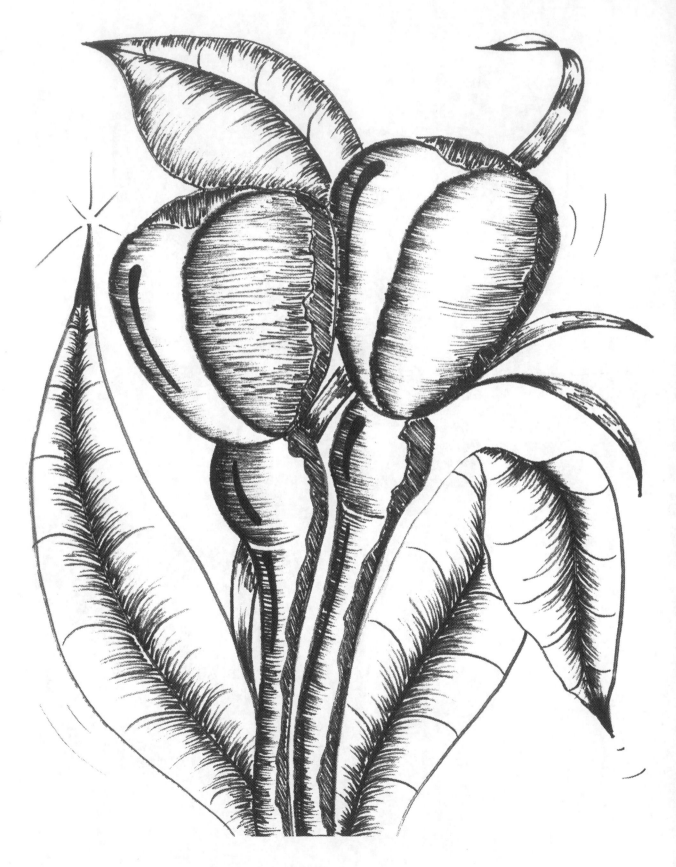

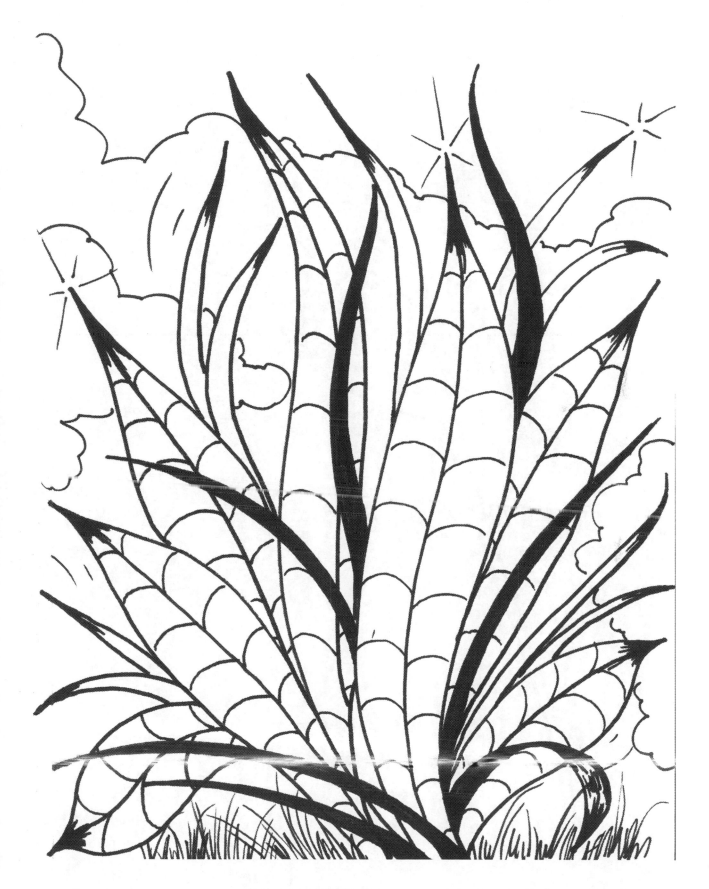

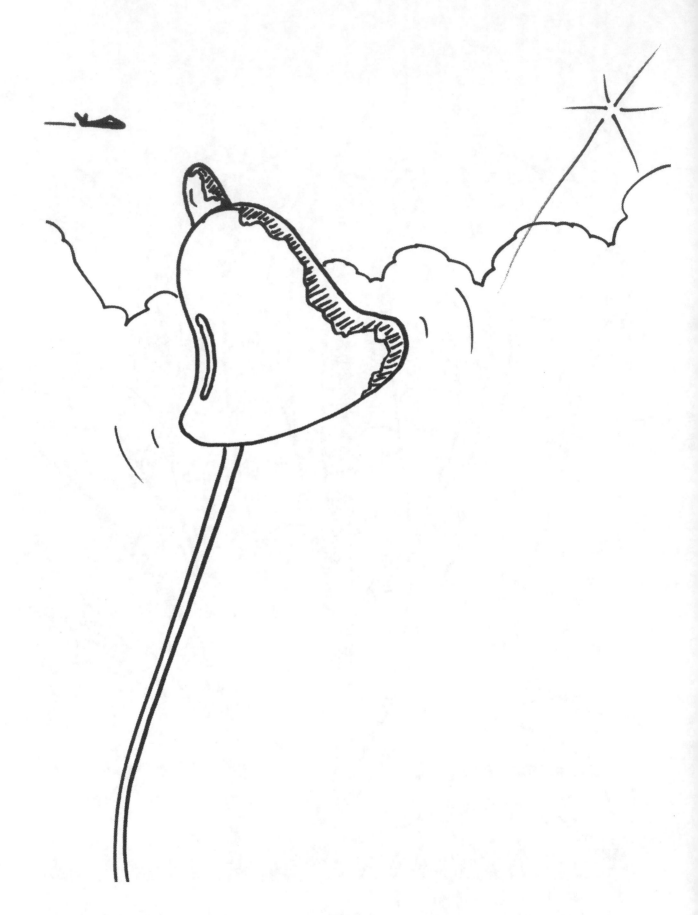

Printed in the United States
By Bookmasters